Dirty, messy, you bet!

Mud pies

Bleck

Sp... ...ing

Tasty finger painting

How to have a messy party

Fossils

Glarch

And that's what makes it so much fun!

Other Marlor Press books for kids:

Kid's Vacation Diary

Kid's Address & Writing Book

Kid's Book to Welcome a New Baby!

Lake Superior, Wow!

Send for free catalog!

Kid's Squish Book

Loris Theovin Bree & Marlin Bree

MARLOR PRESS, INC.

Kid's Squish Book

Copyright 1993 by Loris Theovin Bree & Marlin Bree

Cover design by Georgene Sainati

ISBN 0-943400-76-7
First Edition
Manufactured in the United States of America

Distributed to the book trade by Contemporary Books, Chicago Ill.
and in Canada by Fitzhenry & Whiteside, Ontario

Disclaimer: This book is intended as a book of general activities for kids. Though the authors and the publisher have made best efforts to present helpful information, an adult should insure that the child will have enough help, guidance and supervision to meet specific needs and concerns for welfare and safety. In any event, Marlor Press, Inc., and the authors are not responsible for safety, services, behavior, damage, loss, or injury of any kind.

MARLOR PRESS, INC.
4304 Brigadoon Drive   Saint Paul, MN 55126

Table of Contents

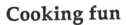

How to prepare for a  SQUISH event

1. Be sure that you are wearing old clothes that are easily washed. It's best if one of your parents tells you that it won't matter if they get all dirty or even stained.

2. Ask Dad or Mom for an old shirt that is no longer being worn by them. Put it on backwards and have someone button it down the back. Then roll up the sleeves so you'll be able to move well.

3. Select your work space. This should be a kitchen or basement area that can easily be cleaned if anything spatters.

4. Find some old newspapers from the recycling bin. Spread them all over the work surface and on the surrounding floor so most of the spatters and mess will go on the paper.

Have fun! BLOOP

Yes!

Button up the back

Old shirt, worn backwards

Sleeves rolled up

Old newspapers spread around to catch spills

(The reason why)

BASIC RECIPES

- Homemade clay for play
- Fun bubbles
- Paste

Homemade clay for play

You'll need

- 2 cups flour

- 2/3 cup salt

- 1 1/2 tablespoon vegetable oil

- 2/3 cup water

1. Put all of the ingredients in a bowl and mix.

2. If the clay seems too stiff, add more water.

3. Store the clay in a plastic bag in your refrigerator.

you can make:

BOWL   RABBIT   FISH

SNAKE

Fun bubbles

You'll need
- 6 cups water

- 1/2 cup liquid dishwashing soap (be sure this is the kind you use for washing dishes by hand, not in a dishwasher)

- 1 tablespoon glycerin

- A big bowl, dish pan or other large container

- A loop or loops of wire

1. Add water first then add the glycerin and then the soap. If you live in a dry climate or it is a dry day, add up to 3 more cups of water. Try to stir carefully and slowly so you won't get any suds.

BLOW GENTLY →

2. Let it sit for a while so any suds will disappear and the ingredients will mix well.

3. Dip the wire loops in the mixture. When you can see that you have a film across the loop, blow gently. You can also buy a "bubble pipe" in some drug stores or dime stores.

Tips:

Certain brands of dishwashing soap seem to work better than others. Some that we've used includes Ajax, Dawn or Joy.

If the bubbles touch something dry they break so have your hands and whatever you are using to make bubbles wet.

Paste

You'll need

- 1 cup white, all-purpose flour

- 1 tablespoon salt

- 1 cup water

- large bowl

- large spoon

1. Put the flour and salt in the bowl.

2. Add the water slowly, stirring as you add. Keep on stirring for a while. The paste should look like whipping cream before it is whipped.

3. Store your paste in the refrigerator. It'll keep for one to two weeks.

you can:

Paste Magazine pictures together

Paste colored papers

Be creative

Different color papers

Paste! Paste!

Paste pictures in Memory Books

NATURALLY YOURS

Mud pies

Fossils

Indoor garden

Bird treats   Volcano

Mud pies

You'll need

- Black dirt that is black or clay-like

- Water

- An old jar cover or other "baking pan"

This is most fun in the spring when it's warm enough to be comfortable outside and when it has recently rained.

MUD
HANDPRINT

1. Find some nice black dirt. The best kind won't have too much sand in it because sand will fall apart when it dries. Second best is clay, but if it's too sticky it may not come out of your "pan." Look for smooth dirt without a lot of sticks and stones in it. Of course, you can always sift the messy stuff out of your dirt. If you can play in a large area, you may want to mix more than one kind of dirt to get just the right mixture.

2. Take an old cup or anything else that will hold water and add water to your dirt or mud until it is just slightly "squishy." It should be easy to mold and should hold its shape but be soft enough to make it fun to work with. In order to get just the right feel, you'll want to mix, pat,

squeeze, let the mud drip through your fingers, try shaping it and then mix some more.

SQUISH SQUISH

3. When the mud feels just right, start shaping it. Make it into pies, cakes, loaves of bread and anything else you can think of. Jar covers, the kind that come on mayonnaise, jam or other foods you buy are just right. If you got your mixture a little too wet, it'll still "bake" nicely.

MUD COOKIE   MUD CAKE (Two-layered)

4. Smooth your pies until they are just the way you want them and then set them in the sun to "bake" outside in the sunlight. On a really warm day the first cakes may be done by the time you finish more. Some days you may need to come back later to see what they look like.

5. Sometimes, you may want to mix up some smooth mud and make frosting.

6. When your cakes are done, you can have a party.

7. DO NOT TRY TO EAT THEM. The fun of this is in making the shapes and seeing them after they are dry. You can have a _pretend_ tea, and invite your friends to _pretend_ they are eating the mud cakes and pies. But, if you get hungry, ask an adult for a cracker or something else that's good to eat. Mud is fun to play with but if you ate it you could get sick.

Fossils

A fossil is the remains of something that was present in the past. Often all that is found is an imprint of something like a leaf or a shell in a rock. Imagine that the leaf or shell landed in a muddy spot and the mud got dry and hard around it. After many, many years the mud turned into rock and the leaf itself disappeared. Today you can still see the pattern it left in the rock.

You'll need

- dirt or clay

- water

1. Find small and interesting stones and pebbles, leaves, pieces of wood, shells or anything you can think of that might make a good fossil.

2. Follow the directions for making a mud pie. Make two pies that look like hamburgers. Put your fossil item on top of one pie and put the other pie on top of the fossil. Then squeeze the two pies together very carefully until you have one thicker pie.

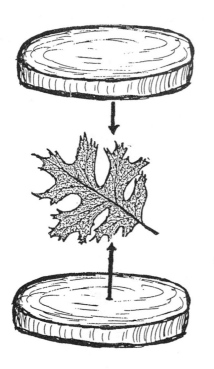

3. When you are sure that your item is completely covered by the pie, set it aside to dry. If is it a warm, sunny day, let it dry for at least one whole day. When it is dry, you can break your mudpie so that you can find the center with the interesting item. When you take out your item you should be able to see its pattern in the mud pie so it looks just like a fossil you might find in a rock.

Indoor gardens

Carrot fern

You'll need

- A fresh plump carrot with some green tops still on it

- A shallow dish

- Clean fresh dirt (preferably potting soil)

- Small rocks or pebbles

- A small clean can that once held 15 to 20 ounces of soup, fruit or vegetables

1. Cut the carrot 1/2 inch down from the top. Cut the green stems and leaves off about 2 inches from the top, leaving a stub. Put the carrot top in the shallow dish and put cold or lukewarm water in the dish so it comes about 1/2 way up the sides of the carrot.

2. Put the dish in a sunny window or under a light where it will get several hours of light every day. Add water every day or every other day so the carrot stays wet. In a few days you should see a lot of new ferns growing.

3. When you have several new fern leaves that are an inch or more long, you can plant the fern in a pot that you make yourself. Pound a nail or other small pointed object into the bottom of the can and make several small holes so the water will drain from your garden. Put some pebbles or small rocks in the bottom of your pot. Then add the black dirt. Put your carrot in the dirt and cover all of the carrot and any roots that have developed with dirt. Just the stems and leaves should show. Now water your new fern and put it back in the light.

4. Want to guess why you put holes and pebbles in the bottom of your planter? That's because you can give plants too much water and the plant might die if it gets too wet. With the pebbles and holes in the bottom, the extra water has a place to drain out of the planter. Be careful to put a dish under the bottom of the planter or to put it in the sink when you give the plant water. You don't want the extra water to run out on a table or window sill and ruin it.

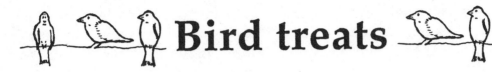

Bird treats

A tree for the birds

During summer and winter the birds will come to visit if you feed them. In an area where it gets cold and snowy, they'll especially appreciate a winter time feast. Use a tree near a window so you can see the birds enjoy your gifts. After Christmas, if you have a tree that is discarded after the holiday, you may want to set it in a snow bank and decorate it for the birds.

You'll need

- Orange halves
- Stale breads, like doughnuts, sweet rolls
- Pretzels
- Stale bread slices
- Suet
- Peanut butter
- Bird seed, grain and nuts
- Yarn
- String, thread, straw
- Lint from the dryer
- Cookie cutters
- Table knife
- Net bags like the kind onions and potatoes come in
- A saucepan or microwave safe glass container
- A wooden spoon for mixing
- An old aluminum foil pie plate

Winter treats

PEANUT BUTTER SLICES. In the winter, birds will enjoy fat to help them keep warm:

1. Use the cookie cutters to cut out shapes from the bread slices.

cookie cutter

Bread slice

2. Spread the shapes with peanut butter.

3. Thread a piece of yarn through the shape and use it to make a loop hanger to hang from the tree. You may use the shapes plain or sprinkle some bird seed in a plate and press the peanut butter into the seed before you hang them.

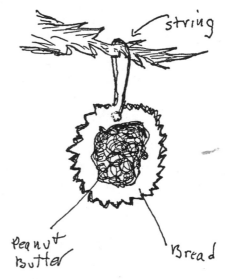

string

Peanut Butter

Bread

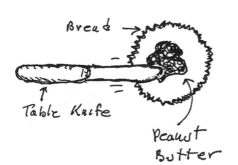

Bread

Table Knife

Peanut Butter

It may take a while for the birds to learn about your tree so be patient, but if you have birds in the area and they're safe from other animals like cats, they'll usually find your tree after a while.

Suet treats

1. With the help of an adult, melt the suet in a saucepan on the stove or in the microwave, being very careful.

Hot!

2. When it is soft and partially melted but not so hot you'll get burned, you may begin working with it (Either melt it and let it cool or only heat it enough to get slightly soft).

Pat Pat

3. Add some of the grain, seed or nuts and mix it with the spoon. You may also add some stale bread pieces, peanut butter or anything else you think the birds will like. When you are sure it won't run anymore, put it into a net bag and hang it from a tree. You may also fill a hollowed out orange half with a mixture like this and hang it from the branches.

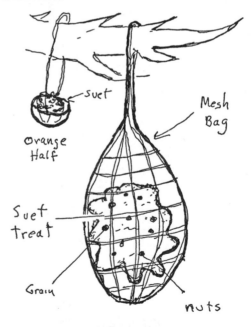

Suet

Orange Half

Mesh Bag

Suet treat

Grain

nuts

Spring treats

When spring comes and the snow starts to melt, birds start to build nests:

1. Fill a net bag with lint from the dryer and with pieces of yarn, straw and string and hang it from your tree. The birds will like to use this material for building nests. They'll also use the yarn pieces that held your wintertime treats.

Summer treats

In the summer, fat spoils more easily and the birds don't need the fat as much so it's better not to use suet and peanut butter but the birds still like to eat:

1. Hang stale doughnuts, sweet rolls, bread slices and pretzels from the tree limbs.

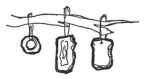

2. Put some bird seed in an old aluminum pie plate, like the kind frozen pies come in, for the birds. Try to wedge it between branches or set it off the ground.

3. Hang an orange half from the tree. Some birds, especially Orioles, like oranges.

Volcano

You'll need

- An empty pop bottle

- 1 tablespoon baking soda

- A large cake pan or similar container

- A mud mixture like the one you used for mud pies

- A glass measuring cup with a lip for pouring

- 1 cup vinegar

1. Rinse out the pop bottle so it is clean. Let it dry thoroughly for a day or two. Then carefully put the baking soda in the bottle.

2. Put the bottle in the cake pan and make a pyramid or mountain shape around it with the mud. Let a half-inch or more of the bottle sick out of the mountain top. Don't get any mud inside of the bottle.

3. Measure the cup of vinegar in the glass measuring cup and carefully pour it into the bottle. Stand back and watch the volcano erupt.

CRAFTY CRAFTS

Beautiful beads
Decoupage treasure box
Decoupage picture
Collage   T-shirt decorating

Beautiful
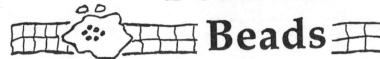
Beads

PEEL

PEEL

You'll need

- A loaf of white bread (day-old bread is great), sliced

- White school glue

- Round toothpicks

- Acrylic paints

- A string

1. Cut or peel off the crust on 10 to 12 bread slices so you only have the white inside left.

2. Pick the white bread into fine pieces or shreds. The smaller the pieces the smoother you beads will be. Put the bread into a mixing bowl.

3. Add enough glue to make a soft dough. There shouldn't be any pieces left that look like bread, you should be able to mix this with your fingers until it seems like clay.

4. With your hands and fingers roll the dough into beads. While it is still sticky, use the toothpicks to punch a hole all the way through each bead.

5. Let dry overnight. Remember these are made with glue and might stick to newspapers. A metal screen or the cooling rack Mom and Dad use to cool baked things might work well. If you dry these on paper, you'll have to turn each of them every few hours until the beads are almost dry so they won't stick to the paper.

6. When the beads are dry, paint them with acrylic paints. Let them dry again.

7. After the beads are dry, put them on the string and make a necklace. You can use a toothpick or a needle to help you poke the string through the beads.

Decoupage treasure box

You'll need

- A cardboard box

- Sealing tape

- An adult helper with a sharp knife

- Lots of white glue

- A paint brush (a small one like you use to paint walls)

- Pretty, colorful pictures from magazines, old greeting cards, comics, wrapping paper or anything else you think will work

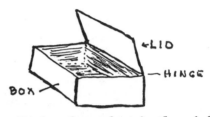

1. Pick a box that is the right size to store your treasures. If you use a corrugated cardboard box, tape the top flaps shut so the empty box is closed, just like it was when something was shipped in it. Set the box so it stands the way you'd like to have your treasure box stand. Then, ask your adult helper to use the sharp knife to cut around three sides of the top, so it will flip open like it had a hinge. Be sure to show the adult which side you want to have hinged.

2. Cut out the colorful pictures. Coat a side of the box with the white glue and lay the colored pictures on them. They should cover all of the box and may overlap just a little (but too much will spoil the appearance of the box.) Continue to coat each side of the box that will show. If you use a corrugated box, you'll probably want the inside of the top flap and the inner sides coated. You might ask your helper to use the sharp knife to trim the sides so they'll come out even.

3. When all the sides have been covered with the pretty pictures, cover it with another coat of white glue. Let it dry thoroughly. Coat with a second layer of white glue and let it dry. You can decide whether you want to add a third layer. When the layers are completely dry you should have a clear, shiny finish over the pictures you selected for your box.

4. Fill your pretty box with treasures you want to save.

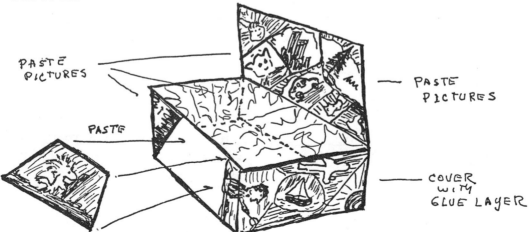

Decoupage picture

You'll need

- See the list of things you'll need on the previous page on *Decoupage treasure box.*

THREE PLATES

1. Use a plain paper plate. Glue a single picture or several pictures in the center of the plate. Leave the edges plain, like a frame for your picture. The picture or pictures should make an attractive image that you would like to have hanging on your wall.

2. Then cover the entire top of the paper plate with the glue. Let dry. Add another layer and let dry.

3. When you have a shiny wall hanging, punch a hole in the top and put a piece of yarn through the hole. Then hang it on your wall.

Collage

You'll need

- White glue

- Heavy paper or cardboard

- Pencil

- Crayons or paints

- Assorted items with textures such as pieces of yarn, wood shavings, seeds, beans, pieces of newspaper or colored magazine, small pieces of cloth, lace, ribbon or anything else that you think might work

1. Use heavy colored or white paper or lightweight cardboard cut in the size and shape you want for your picture. With a pencil draw a picture on the paper.

Collage is a picture with texture made by using items that usually might not be found in pictures.

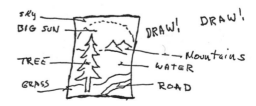

2. Decide where you want your textured material. Cover that area with glue and then fill it with the material you want to use.

For example, you might want to use:

- Green yarn for the leaves of a tree

- Wood shavings for a house.

You may want to soak pieces of ribbon, yarn or fabric in glue to be sure it will stick.

3. Fill in parts of your picture with crayon or paint. When it is thoroughly dry, hang the picture on your wall or give it to a friend.

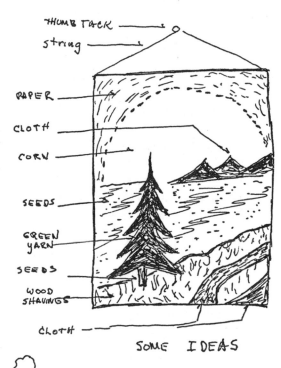

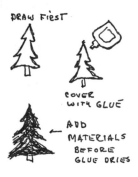

T-shirt decorating

You'll need

- A plain T-shirt of any color

- Permanent felt-tip markers, crayons, fabric markers or fabric paint

- A plain piece of paper

1. If the T-shirt is wrinkled, ask your adult helper to press it so it'll be smooth when you paint it.

2. Insert the plain paper inside the shirt, between the front and back, so the color won't bleed through. Use your choice of paint and design.

Drawn on

pressed T-shirt

Hand print

3. You can use markers or crayons to draw:

- a picture of a pet

- Your family

- Your school

- Or a favorite character from a book.

You also can write your name, the name of your school or the name of your favorite team. You can dip your hand in fabric paint and then put your hand print on the shirt.

4. Another idea is dip your fingers in fabric paint, put fingerprints on the shirt and then use crayons or markers to draw bodies, hair, etc. on the fingerprints, making them into little people or animals.

5. If you use crayons or fabric paint you'll probably have to have an adult helper make the design more permanent by setting it with an iron. Follow the directions that come with the fabric paint or put another piece of cloth over the crayon drawing and press it with the iron set on "wool" for 30 to 60 seconds.

SLIGHTLY MESSY PAINTING

Splatter painting   Tasty finger painting

Squishy, but not messy finger painting

Earth paints   Impasto

Sand painting

Splatter painting

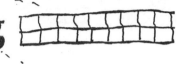

You'll need

- Paint—water colors, poster paint, or your own natural paints
  A clean piece of screen

- White paper or contrasting color paper

- An old toothbrush that is no longer being used

- Leaves—some that have fallen from your favorite tree would be great

1. After you've put on your paint shirt and spread newspapers all around, arrange the leaves on your white paper. Just one or two leaves is fine. You want to be able to see the outline of each leaf.

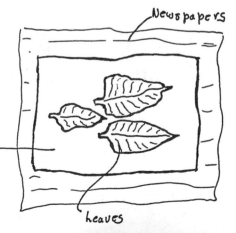

Newspapers

White paper

leaves

2. Dip the toothbrush in the paint. Then, hold the screen an inch or two above the paper and rub the toothbrush carefully over the top of the screen. Your paper will soon be covered with splatters of paint.

3. When you have enough splatters, carefully lay down your screen and toothbrush and lift the leaf. You'll see a pretty leaf design surrounded by splatters.

4. Clean your screen and toothbrush before you put them away with the paints.

5. Let your splatter painting dry and hang it in your room or give it to someone special.

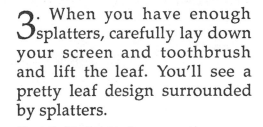

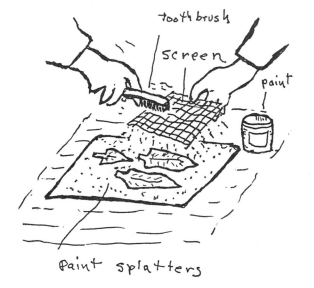

Paint splatters

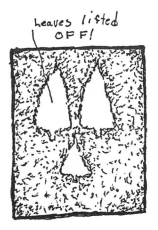

Leaves lifted OFF!

Tasty finger painting

SHAKE! SHAKE!

You'll need

- Chocolate instant pudding (4 serving size)

- 2 cups cold milk

- White paper

- Quart jar with lid

- Small flat bowl

- Paper

FUN

1. Find a quart jar with a tight lid. Put your pudding and milk in the jar and shake it hard until the pudding is well mixed. You'll need to shake it for one or two minutes but don't shake it too long or it won't get thick. Pour the pudding into a small flat bowl like a large cereal dish. Let the pudding sit for 5 minutes until it gets thick.

or

Follow the directions on the box to mix the pudding and thicken it.

2. Lay your paper on news-papers. Put on your paint shirt and finger paint.

4. When you have a picture you like, set the picture aside to dry and do another.

3. Dip your fingers in the chocolate pudding and then run your fingers over the paper. Your paper should be covered with just a little chocolate pudding. Now you can make lines, circles, swirls, wavy lines and other designs with your fingers in the pudding.

5. When you finish, wash your hands, clean up your dish and throw out the dirty newspapers.

6. When your picture is dry, hang it in your room or give it to someone you like.

Squishy but not messy finger painting

You'll need

- 6 Tablespoons of liquid laundry starch *

- 4 Tablespoons of powdered tempera paint

- One gallon-size resealable clear plastic bag

When buying starch, be sure to get the thick cloudy kind that comes in a big bottle. The clear spray starch won't work. You may have to look around for the right kind because not every grocery store carries it.

1. Put the starch and paint into a gallon-size zipper (reseal- able) plastic bag.

SQUISH

SQUISH

2. Press the top of the bag to get the air out before you carefully seal the bag. Then put some masking tape across the seal and around the edges to be sure it is very tight shut.

3. Squeeze the bag carefully to mix the paint and starch.

4. Now lay the bag flat on a table and use your fingers and your hands to make pictures. You erase them by running your hands across the bag to make it smooth again. Turn on the radio or your audio player to listen to music while you make pictures.

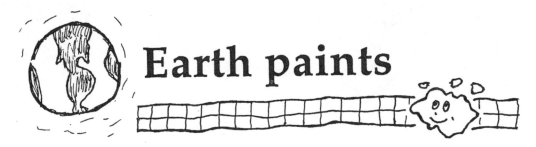

Earth paints

You'll need

- Soil
- Bowl
- Containers
- Newspaper
- Baby food jars or other small jars
- Plastic bag
- Paintbrushes
- Hammer
- Water
- Sieve
- Paper

1. Look for soil of different colors. It's best if the soil comes from an area without a lot of vegetation and that is not too sandy. You'll have to look in different places to find different colors but if you keep looking, you'll find colors that range from yellow and brown to red-brown to almost black.

2. Whenever you find a new color, put it in a container (like a can, pan or jar) and take it home. Then spread it on a newspaper until it is very dry.

3. Put the dried soil into a plastic bag—a heavy bag or a double bag works best. Take the bag and a hammer outside or to a work bench where you can pound without hurting anything. Pound the lumps until they are broken up and you have fine dirt.

4. Put your sieve over a bowl or newspaper and put the dirt through the sieve so that you only have the finest and smoothest soil left to save. Put the fine dry soil in small jars and store until you are ready to paint.

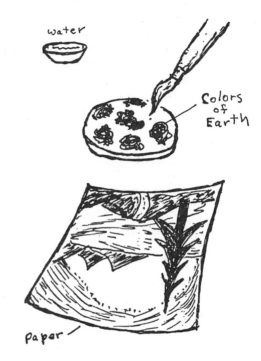

5. When you are ready to paint, put a small amount of earth on a plate and mix in a few drops of water until you have a paint-like paste. Use a paintbrush to begin to paint your picture. Continue with other colors of soil. You may paint your picture on paper, rocks or wood.

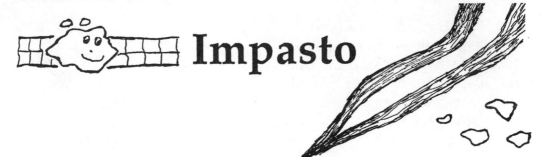

Impasto

You'll need

- Containers for mixing

- Liquid starch (see the note on page 32)

- Dry tempera paint

- Colored paper

- Heavy artist's paint brush

- Objects to draw with (pointed stick, popsicle stick, comb, plastic fork, anything that will make a mark in the thick layers of paint)

Impasto is the process of applying thick layers of paint to a surface

1. Mix the liquid starch and paint until you have a thick but fluffy mixture. This works best with at least two or three colors.

MIX

MIX

containers
for storing

2. Brush a heavy layer over the paper. Using one of the objects, draw a design in the paint. Allow the paint to dry.

MORE LAYERS

FIRST LAYER

DRAW!
DRAW!

LAYER 2

LAYER 3

LAYER 4

LAYER 5

3. Then paint another color in your design over the background color. You can also use a popsicle stick to put patches of paint on the paper so it looks like an oil painting.

4. If you want to, you may allow the paint to dry between layers and add more layers and more colors.

Sand painting

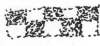

You'll need

- White school glue

- Fine dry sand—like the kind you find at the beach

- Heavy paper or cardboard

- Newspaper to catch the sand

- Crayons

1. Lay the paper or cardboard on the newspaper. Use the pointed tip of the school glue bottle like a pencil and draw a design on the paper (Some people think they get a nicer picture if they draw the design first with a pencil). Sprinkle the sand over the wet glue and then tip the paper so that all of the sand that doesn't stick to the glue will slide off onto the newspaper.

2. Let the sand and glue dry and then use your crayons to draw other colors and highlights on your sand painting.

DRAW! DRAW! GLUE

SPRINKLE SAND

ADD FLOWERS

color

RECYCLED

STUFF

◇ **Lint paper**
▷ **Finger painting**
◇ **Another kind of finger painting**

Lint paper

You'll need

- Lots of lint from the clothes dryer. (Save it for several days if you have your own dryer or gather quite a bit from the laundromat.)
- Tiny pieces of colored tissue paper, colored paper, newspaper, cloth, thread, dried flower petals, dried leaves or dried grasses.
- Cake pan (round or square)
- Soft absorbent cloth
- Construction paper
- Cookie sheet
- Metal sheers
- Old screen or wire mesh
- Water
- White Glue

1. With metal sheers, cut the screen or mesh so it fits easily into the cake pan.

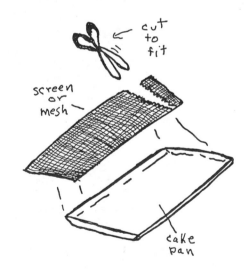

2. Put the wire mesh in the cake pan. Add lint and any other materials (paper, thread, fabric or leaves). Then add warm water. Be sure everything is wet. Let soak for 10 minutes.

4. Move your dry lint paper from the screen to a contrasting piece of construction paper. Glue to the paper. When you get an especially pretty piece, you may want to frame it.

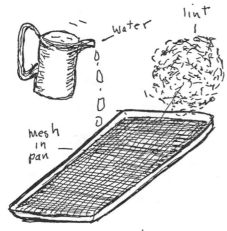

soak lint in tray

3. Lift the wire mesh out of the mixture carefully so that a layer of lint and materials is on top. Put it on a dish drainer or cookie sheet to drain. Carefully blot the lint layer with the absorbent cloth. Then let dry.

 # Finger paints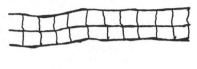

You'll need

- Enough pieces of old bar soap to make 1/2 cup soap chips
- 3/4 cup cornstarch
- 5 cups water
- Large sauce pan or large glass container for the microwave
- Wooden spoon or other large spoon for stirring
- Food coloring or pieces of colored chalk
- Old margarine containers with lids or other recycled containers that can be covered
- Small spoon or spoons
- Paper

1. You'll need adult help for this because the mixture gets very hot. In the saucepan or microwave dish, mix the finely chipped soap, cornstarch and water. Bring the mixture to a boil. If you're cooking over a stove, the mix needs to be stirred constantly. If you're cooking in the microwave, cook the mixture for 2 minutes, take it out and stir, then cook for two more minutes. Continue until done.

2. When the mixture is thick, remove it allow it to cool slightly and then pour it into the individual containers while still quite warm. Add a different color of coloring or chalk to each container and mix each one with a small clean spoon.

paper

Paint! Paint!

Paints in containers

3. If you use the same spoon for each one, rinse it off and dry between each color or chalk. Let the mixtures sit until cool.

4. Cover the containers and store until you're ready to use them. Then use the colors like any fingerpaints, putting a little bit on paper and making designs with your hands and fingers.

Another kind of finger paint

This is only recycling if you've already purchased the materials to use in other projects.

You'll need

- Paper
- That big bottle of liquid starch you purchased to use in Not Messy Finger Painting and Glarch
- Extra tempera paint or food coloring

1. Pour a little liquid starch on the paper. Add some paint or food coloring.

2. Mix the color and starch with your fingers on the paper and then make the designs and swirls you like with your hands and fingers.

COOKING FUN

Homemade peanut butter   **Caramel apples**

Bread figures   **Soft pretzels**

Burger dinner   **Caramel popcorn balls**

Note: Cooking almost always involves handling hot dishes and food. Children should have an adult assistant to help with the hot things or they should be older and have a parent's permission to try these recipes on their own.

 # Homemade peanut butter

You'll need

- A blender or food processor

- About 13 ounces or 2 1/2 cups salted peanuts

- 1 ounce or 2 tablespoons of cooking oil (peanut oil or canola oil are best)

- Rubber scraper

- A jar large enough to hold 1 cup of peanut butter

1. Put peanuts in the blender or food processor. Cover and blend until they are chopped.

2. Add the oil to the chopped peanuts. Cover and blend at a low speed while you slowly count to ten (about 10 seconds). Turn off the blender or food processor, take off the cover and use the scraper to scrape down the sides.

3. Put on the cover and process on low speed while you slowly count to five (5 seconds). Turn off the blender, take off the cover and scrape down the sides.

scrape down sides
when blender is OFF!

4. Repeat the last step 3 or 4 more times until it starts to look like peanut butter. Cover and blend at a high speed for about 1 minute.

5. Scrape the peanut butter from the blender into the jar. Put it in the refrigerator for at least an hour before you use it.

yum! Good stuff!
My Own PEANUT BUTTER

If you like crunchy peanut butter instead of smooth,

A. Measure out 1/2 cup of peanuts before you start the first step. Save them to use later.

B. Follow steps 1, 2, 3, and 4.

C. Take off the cover of the blender and add the 1/2 cup of whole peanuts. Cover the blender and blend at medium speed while you slowly count to three (about 3 seconds).

D. Follow step 5.

 Caramel apples

You'll need

- 6 medium sized apples (a crisp hard apple like Granny Smith works best)

- 6 wooden ice-cream sticks

- 14 to 16 ounces of vanilla caramels

- 3 tablespoons water

- a double boiler (for the stove) or a large glass measuring dish or other big glass dish(for the microwave)

- waxed paper

- long handled spoon

1. Pull out 6 squares of waxed paper and put them on your work table.

2. Wash the 6 apples and dry them. Push an ice cream stick into the end of each apple.

3. Unwrap the caramels and put them in the top of the double boiler (if you're using a stove) or in the large glass dish (if you are using a microwave). Add 3 tablespoons of water to the unwrapped candy.

4. Put hot water in the bottom of the double boiler and put it on a burner of the stove. Put the top on the double boiler. Heat the double

boiler with the caramels over medium heat. As the candy starts to melt, stir it with the long handled spoon. Stir until the caramels are melted and the mixture is smooth, about 20 to 25 minutes.

or

If you have a microwave, put the glass dish containing the caramels in the microwave. Microwave at high for 3 or 4 minutes. Then take the dish out and stir the caramels. Return the mixture to the microwave and cook on high for 2 or 3 minutes until the candy can be stirred smooth.

5. Put the hot caramel on the table and very carefully dip each apple in the hot caramel mix. This is going to be *very* hot so it's good to have an adult assistant to help. While the apple is still in the caramel, use the spoon to dip into the mixture and pour it over the part that doesn't get covered.

6. After it is dipped, put each apple on a square of waxed paper. When you are finished, put the apples in the refrigerator for an hour or more until the caramel is cold.

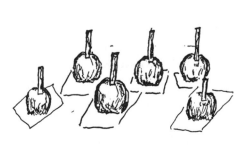

Bread figures

You'll need

- 1 loaf of frozen bread dough
- A little flour
- 1/4 cup milk
- 1 tablespoon of soft butter or margarine plus some for the baking sheet
- 2 tablespoons honey
- Cookie sheet
- A place to roll out the dough
- A rolling pin
- 2 cups
- Small bowl
- Fork
- White paper
- Pencil
- Paper scissors
- Kitchen scissors
- Pancake turner
- A wire rack for cooling your figures
- Pastry brush or spoon

1. Thaw the loaf of bread. Either let it sit in the refrigerator overnight or at room temperature just until thawed.

2. With the pencil and paper, draw patterns for animal figures. Simple outlines of animals are best. Some suggestions might be a dog, a cat, an owl, a goose, a gingerbread style boy or girl, an alligator, an elephant. Cut out the pattern with paper scissors. Make about 6 small patterns.

STAR

OWL

3. When you are ready to start, turn the oven on and set the temperature at 350 degrees F. Grease the cookie sheet with butter or margarine.

4. Put about 1/4 cup flour in a cup. Pour 1/4 cup milk into another cup. Set these aside to use.

5. Make sure your work table is very clean and dry. Then sprinkle the flour on it and put your thawed bread dough on it.

6. Using the rolling pin, roll the thawed dough into a rectangle about 10 inches long and 8 inches wide.

7. Put just a few drops of milk on the dough and then put the pattern on the damp dough. Cut around the pattern with the kitchen scissors.

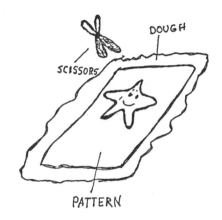

DOUGH

SCISSORS

PATTERN

8. Use the pancake turner to carefully move the dough figure to the cookie sheet. Peel off the pattern and use your fingers to change the shape of your figure. If you'd like to add eyes, hair, tail or other decorations, cut little pieces from the scraps that were left after you cut out your figures. Dip the pieces in milk to make them stick better.

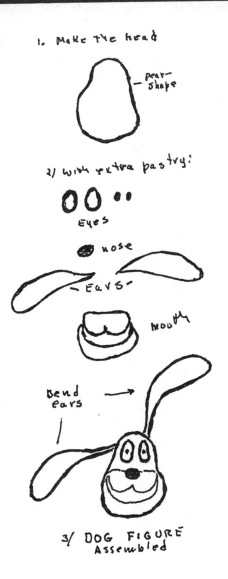

1. Make the head

pear-shape

2/ with extra pastry:

Eyes

nose

- Ears -

mouth

bend ears →

3/ DOG FIGURE Assembled

9. When you have finished the figures, ask your adult helper to put them in the hot oven. Bake them for 15 to 20 minutes until they are light brown.

10. While the figures are baking, put the 1 tablespoons butter or margarine and the 2 tablespoons honey in the small bowl. Use the fork to mix them together until the mixture looks like whipped butter.

11. When the figures are baked, have your helper remove them from the oven and, using the pancake turner, carefully put each figure on the wire rack.

12. Using a pastry brush or spoon, spread some of the honey butter over each figure. Let them cool and then eat them, unless they're too pretty.

Soft pretzels

You'll need

- 1 loaf of frozen bread dough, thawed

- 1 egg or 1 egg white and 1 teaspoon water

- Coarse salt

- Small amount of butter or margarine

- Cookie sheet

- Pastry brush or spoon

- Pancake turner

- Wire rack for cooling

1. Beat the egg in a cup or small dish.

2. Knead the bread dough and then cut into 8 pieces.

3. Turn the oven on and set the temperature at 350 degrees F. Grease the cookie sheet.

4. Wash and dry your hands, then pick up one of the pieces of dough and roll it between your hands into long narrow ropes. Twist the ropes into shapes like pretzels or any other shape you like. Put the dough on the greased cookie sheet, leaving some space between each pretzel.

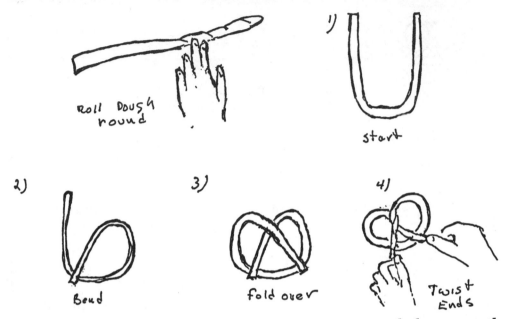

Roll Dough round

1) start

2) Bend

3) fold over

4) Twist Ends

5. When you have finished the eight pretzels, brush on the beaten egg. If you don't have a pastry brush, use the spoon to drip some egg on your pretzel and use your fingers to brush it around the top of your dough. Then sprinkle coarse salt over the pretzel.

6. Have your helper put the cookie sheet with the pretzels in the hot oven. Bake for 10 to 15 minutes until the shape is golden brown.

7. When the pretzels are brown have your helper take them out of the oven and cool on a wire rack until they are cool or only slightly warm. Then you invite a friend to eat pretzels with you.

Burger dinner packages

You'll need

- 1 pound ground beef
- 1/2 to 3/4 teaspoon seasoning salt
- 1 medium sized onion or 1/2 large onion
- 2 medium potatoes
- 2 carrots
- salt
- pepper
- 4 tablespoons catsup
- Aluminum foil
- Mixing bowl
- Large baking dish (13 x 9 x 2 inches or larger)
- Sharp knife
- Vegetable peeler

1. Turn the oven on and set the temperature at 375 degrees.

2. Tear off four big squares of aluminum foil. Then wash your hands carefully. Put the ground beef in the mixing bowl and mix it with the seasoning salt. Make four piles of ground beef on each square of aluminum foil. They should all be about the same size. Then make each pile into a round hamburger patty about 3/4 inch thick.

HAMBURGER

Foil

3. Peel the onion and ask your helper to help you cut it into slices. There should be at least one slice on each burger. Peel the two potatoes and ask you helper to cut each into thin slices. Put about half of a potato on top of the onion slices. Measure 1 tablespoons of catsup and put on the potatoes on each of the squares.

4. Peel the carrots and ask your helper to slice them in thin slices. Put about half of a carrot on top of the potatoes and catsup. Measure about 1/8 teaspoon of salt and sprinkle over the vegetables. Sprinkle just a little pepper on top of the vegetables.

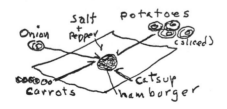

5. Bring two sides of foil up above the food. Press the top edges together and then make a fold of about 1/2 inch, then fold over again and again until the fold is down to the top of the food. Fold over tightly against the food. Then press the unfolded edges together and crease into a point. Fold up tightly against the food.

6. Put the foil package into the large pan. Put the pan in the oven and bake it for 1 hour and 20 minutes. Put a package on each plate and let everyone open their own package. Tell them to be very careful because the packages are filled with hot steam.

Caramel popcorn balls

You'll need

- 5 cups popped corn

- 1/2 lb caramels

- 2 tablespoons water

- double boiler or large glass microwave safe dish

- large spoon

- large bowl or very clean dishpan

- Waxed paper

1. Unwrap the caramels and put them in the top of the double boiler (if you're using a stove) or in the large glass dish (if you are using a microwave). Add 3 tablespoons of water to the unwrapped candy.

2. Put hot water in the bottom of the double boiler and put it on a burner of the stove. Put the top on the double boiler. Heat the double boiler with the caramels over medium heat. As the candy starts to melt, stir it with the long handled spoon. Stir until the caramels are melted and the mixture is smooth, about 20 to 25 minutes.

or

If you have a microwave, put the glass dish containing the caramels in the microwave. Microwave at high for 3 or 4 minutes. Then take the dish out and stir the caramels. Return the mixture to the microwave and cook on high for 2 or 3 minutes until the candy can be stirred smooth.

3. Put the popped corn in a large bowl or dishpan so that you can stir it without spilling popcorn.

4. Pour the melted caramel mixture over the popcorn, a little bit at a time. Stir the mixture with the wooden spoon after each time you pour. (An adult helper can be very useful for this step.)

5. After the caramel and popcorn are mixed, wash your hands with soap and water. Dry them well and check the popcorn mixture to be sure it's not too hot to handle. As soon as you can comfortably handle it, make balls by squeezing the caramel covered popcorn together with your hands until you have a popcorn ball that is the right size.

6. Put it on the waxed paper and make another one until you have used up all of the popcorn. Share these with friends and your family.

DETECTIVE WORK

WHO DID IT?

Making fingerprints

Finding a fingerprint

Tracing footprints and other impressions

Making fingerprints

You'll need

- A black ink pad

- A white sheet of paper

- Soft black lead pencil

- Fine sandpaper

- A soft paintbrush

 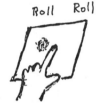

1. Rub your fingertip over the ink pad. Then roll your finger over the white paper.

2. Have other friends or family members also make their finger-prints. Write the name of the person who made the fingerprint beside each one. This is your "fingerprint file."

3. Look at the fingerprints. Is there a way that they are all alike? How are they different? No finger-prints are ever alike but they may have similar patterns.

4. Come back into the room and compare the unknown fingerprint with the ones in your file. See if you can find a print in your file that looks just like the new one. Were you right?

3. Now, while you leave the room, ask one of the others to make a fingerprint with the same finger they used for your "fingerprint file." Ask your friends not to tell you who made the last print.

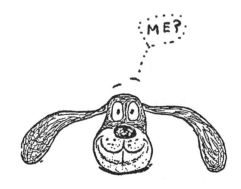

ME?

Finding a fingerprint

You'll need

- A lead pencil

- A piece of fine sandpaper

- Paintbrush

- A glass, dish or other shiny surface which has been handled by another person

1. Rub the lead part of your pencil on the fine sandpaper. Did you know that the part you write with is actually graphite, not lead? Save the graphite powder.

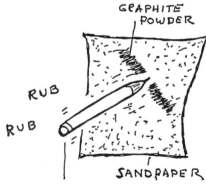

2. Take a glass that has just been used by someone. With the paintbrush, brush some graphite powder over the glass. The powder should stick to oil from the finger left on the glass.

3. Did you find a fingerprint? Can you see a pattern of lines left by the finger?

GRAPHITE POWDER

PAINTBRUSH

GLASS

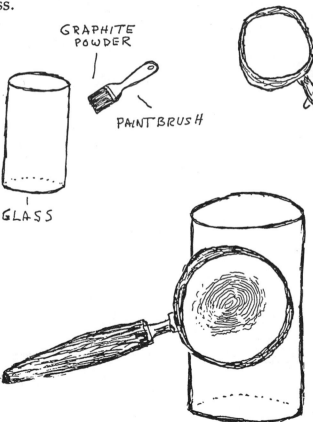

Look closely: It's a fingerprint!

Tracing footprints and other impressions

You'll need

- Plaster of Paris

- Dish

- Water

- Spoon

- A long strip of cardboard, about 1 inch wide

- A pin or paper clip

Sometimes police find tire tracks, foot prints or unusual indentations at the scene of a crime. If they think the impressions might be important, they want to keep a record of them so they can compare them with the actual shoes or tires.

1. Find a spot that is or has been muddy, where a footprint or tire print has made a clear impression.

FOOT PRINT.   TIRE PRINT

2. Make a big circle of the cardboard and pin or clip the ends together. Put the cardboard ring around the indentation. It should be big enough to circle the entire footprint or impression. If any pebbles or loose pieces of dirt are laying inside the indented area, take them out. Be very careful so that you don't disturb the marks you want to copy.

CARDBOARD
RING

3. Put some plaster of Paris in the dish and slowly add water. Stir with the spoon. Add enough water to make a smooth, thick, creamy mixture.

4. Pour the Plaster of Paris mixture into the cardboard ring.

POUR
POUR

5. As soon as the mixture has hardened, take it out of the cardboard ring. When it is completely dry, you can wash it if there is any mud or dirt left on it. Now you'll have a clear copy of your impression.

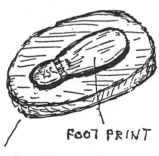

FOOT PRINT

CAST

6. If you found the indentation near your home, you may want to check to see if it was left by someone in your own family. Look in the closets of any member of the family that will let you and see if you find a shoe that matches the plaster footprint.

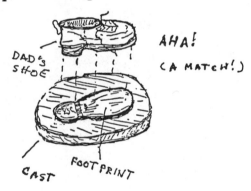

DAD's SHOE

AHA!

(A MATCH!)

CAST

FOOTPRINT

7. Or, check the tires on the family auto to see if your tire print matches.

CAST

TIRE TRACK

ANOTHER MATCH!

8. If you live near a wooded area, or where there is water or a park, look for animal tracks and follow the same steps to make a casting of animal tracks.

MOUSE

FOX

CHIPMUNK

SQUIRREL

HUMAN

(in shoes)

AHA!

WEIRD STUFF

Glarch
Bleck
Oobleck   Glob

Note: All of the weird stuff is water soluble and will wash out of clothing or off of floors and furniture.

Glarch

Kids love these unusual mixtures and they'll think of all sorts of ways to use them that adults never would. A great way to be creative.

You'll need

- 4 ounces white school glue
- 1/4 cup liquid starch (*see note below)

- Food coloring

In buying starch, be sure to get the thick cloudy kind that comes in a big bottle. The clear spray starch won't work. You may have to look around for the right kind because not every grocery store carries it.

1. Drain school glue into bowl. Add liquid starch and food coloring. Mix well with your hands or a spoon or fork. If the mixture is too sticky, add a little more starch.

2. Use your imagination in playing with this. It's all sorts of fun to pull it apart and squeeze it back together in different shapes. It'll get stringy and then will go back together in a lump if you let it sit for a while.

3. This doesn't store well, even in a plastic bag in the refrigerator, so make it the day you plan to use it.

Bleck

You'll need

- Jelly roll pan or other large baking sheet with sides

- 1 cup corn starch

- 1 1/2 cups water

- Bowl

1. Mix the corn starch and water together in the bowl and pour into the jelly roll pan.

2. Let the mixture sit in the jelly roll pan until the corn starch settles to the bottom and the water is on top (1/2 hour to 1 hour).

3. Draw, write or make pictures in the mixture using your fingers. If it gets all mixed up, let it set for a while until it settles. If the water evaporates or gets splashed out, just add more water.

 # Oobleck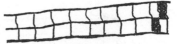

You'll need

- A flat plastic refrigerator container, large enough for you to easily slip your hands inside and handle the oobleck
- 1 cup of cornstarch
- 1/2 cup of water
- A fork

This is a strange and mysterious mixture.

1. Put the cornstarch in the container. Add the water and stir it carefully with the fork. Be careful and keep stirring even though it seems stiff and hard.

2. When this mixture is thoroughly mixed, you'll have Oobleck. It should drip from your fork or fingers but it should also be solid if you try to poke a finger into it. If it seems too dry, add a drop or more of water. If is too runny, let it sit for a few hours and then stir it again.

3. Mix it with the fork and let it drip through the tines of the fork. Drag your fingers or the fork through the mixture and make a path. Try to put your hand or fingers through the mixture. Let the mixture sit for a minute, then stick the fork in and scoop it out. See what other things you can do with it. Ask yourself, is this a liquid or a solid? How do you know?

Have you ever seen such a strange mixture?

Glob

You'll need

- 2 bowls
- 4 ounces white school glue
- Food coloring*
- 1 teaspoon borax*
- 1 cup water
- A spoon

This is much like *Glarch* but we think it seems a little smoother.

1. Pour the school glue and 1/2 cup water into a bowl. Mix the two ingredients together. Add just a few drops of food coloring.

2. Put 1/2 cup water in another bowl. Add 1 teaspoon borax and mix well. Pour the glue mixture into the borax mixture and mix.

3. You should have a thick mass in a liquid. When the glob seems to have formed into one chunk, pour off the rest of the liquid. You can make the mixture thicker and drier by kneading, stretching and playing with it.

4. Let the mixture slowly pour from your hands back into the bowl and see how it flows. Then, try to pull it apart quickly and see how it breaks. When it gets drier, it will start to bounce. What else can you make it do?

* If you don't have food coloring, you'll still have glob but it'll be white glob. Borax is a washing powder found in the laundry section of most grocery stores.

PAPIER-MACHE

Bracelet
Napkin rings
Piggy bank

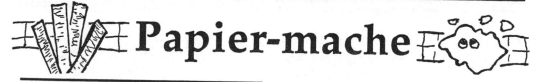

Papier-mache

You'll need

- A large plastic garbage bag
- Lots of newspapers
- A big dish for your paste
- Flour
- Water
- Salt

OINK

Papier-mache is wonderfully messy and can be used to make all kinds of projects. Be sure to spread lots of newspapers around the room where you'll be working before you start.

For easy cleanup, tear open the plastic bag and tape it to your work table. If you cover the table with newspapers, your papier-mache project is likely to stick to it.

To make a paste

Mix 1 cup of flour with 1 tablespoon salt. Add 1 1/2 cups of water or more. The paste should feel like thick cream. Add more water or flour until the paste seems about right.

How to do papier-mache

1. Tear the newspapers into strips. It's just fine to have the strips be in uneven sizes, but about 1 inch wide and 5 inches long is about right for long, open areas. Use small pieces of paper for sharp corners and tiny areas. Use large pieces for large and rounded areas. Strips you tear work better than strips cut with a scissors because the scissors' straight edges will show through.

2. Dip the strips in the paste so both sides are covered. Let the extra paste drip off, or just use your thumb and a finger to remove it. Now put the pasted strips, one at a time, over the base. Overlap the strips just a little and keep putting them on the base until it is covered with a single layer of paste and newspaper. Although you want to overlap the strips a bit, you don't want any place where there are several layers of strips that are all wet.

NEWSPAPER STRIPS

DIP IN PASTE

OVERLAP STRIPS

3. Let the layer dry before you add another layer. This will take at least a day and may take longer.

4. When the first layer is thoroughly dry, add a second layer. When you do the new layer, lay the strips in a different direction and at an angle from the first ones.

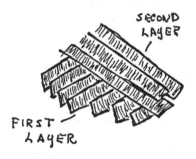

SECOND LAYER

FIRST LAYER

5. If you use the newspapers' colored comic strips for the second layer, you'll be able to tell that you have completely covered the first layer with the second layer. Always let each layer dry thoroughly before you do the next one. You'll probably want three or four layers if you have a solid base and six or seven layers if you're making a hollow model, like the piggy bank.

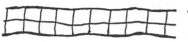 # Bracelet

You'll need

- Lightweight cardboard like a cereal box
- Scissors
- Ruler
- Pencil
- Masking tape
- Paste
- Newspapers

1. Flatten your cardboard. Use the ruler to measure a strip 9 to 10 inches long. Mark a straight line with your pencil and then mark another straight line 3/4 inch to 1 inch wide. Cut out the strip with the scissors.

RULER / CUT / card board —

TAPE ENDS TOGETHER

2. Make a circle out of the cardboard, lapping the ends by 1/2 inch. Tape the ends together and try on the bracelet. It should be loose now because it will be smaller when you have the papier-mache layers added. When it is just right, tape lots of masking tape on it so it'll stay together.

3. Tear narrow, short strips of newspaper, about 1/2 inch wide and 2 inches long. Begin laying the paper on the band. Always allow each layer to get thoroughly dry and put each layer at different angles to make it stronger. You'll want about three layers.

— PAPER STRIP

LAYERS

PAINT AND DECORATE!

Napkin rings

You'll need

These will be great to use for family meals.

- 2 toilet paper tubes instead of the flat cardboard

- The same materials used for the bracelet

1. Flatten each tube and cut it into three rings 1 1/2 inches wide.

2. Follow the directions for the bracelet, covering each of the six rings with a layer of paper and paste and letting them dry before you begin the next layer. Then decorate them.

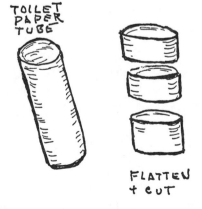

TOILET
PAPER
TUBE

FLATTEN
+ CUT

PAPER
STRIP

COVER

DECORATE

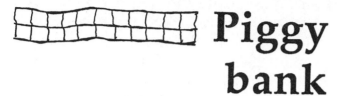

Piggy bank

You'll need

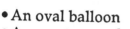

- An oval balloon
- An empty metal can
- Cooking oil
- Masking tape
- 3 toilet paper tubes
- Paste
- Scissors
- Newspapers
- A piece of corrugated cardboard from a box or box top
- A small piece of bendable wire
- A sharp craft knife

1. Blow up the balloon and cover it with a thin layer of oil. Put the tied end in the empty metal can so it will sit quietly while you work. The oil will make it easier to collapse your balloon foundation without collapsing your pig. Work carefully so you won't make the balloon burst before you want it to.

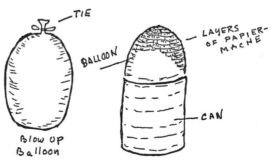

2. Following the directions for basic papier-mache, paste two layers all over the balloon and let them dry.

3. To make legs, flatten two toilet paper tubes and cut them in half. Now, make the four pieces round again and tape them to your papier-mache covered balloon. With masking tape, tape the legs to one side of the balloon. Be sure you use a big side of the balloon so it'll look like a pig. Set the pig on the table and adjust the legs so it stands up.

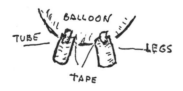

4. Flatten the last tube and cut a piece a little shorter than the legs to make a nose. Tape the nose to the end

opposite the tied end you put in the can. Stuff the tubes with crumpled newspaper and tape them shut with masking tape so you'll have a flat end.

5. Cut two rounded triangles from the cardboard to make ears. Then cut a "V" into the middle of the wide end and tape it so you'll have a curved ear.

6. Tape the wire to the end opposite the nose, making it into a loop so it'll look like a curly tail.

7. Continue to add more layers, covering the legs, nose, ears and tail. You'll probably only want about two layers on the ears and tail.

8. When you have six or seven dry layers over the balloon you are almost finished. Using a pin, poke through all of the layers and pop the balloon. Then ask an adult to cut a coin slot in the top of your pig with a sharp craft knife.

CUT SLOT IN TOP

9. Next, it's time to paint your pig. Follow the painting directions and don't forget to add eyes in a different color.

How to paint your creations

You'll need

- Inexpensive artist's paint brushes
- Paint (tempera, acrylic, poster)

You may also want:

- Pencil
- Magic Marker
- White Waterproof Glue (not school glue)

1. After your project is thoroughly dry, decide how you'll want it to look. If you want it to be washable, you'll need to use waterproof paint. Acrylic paint or tempera mixed with waterproof glue is best. Regular tempera or poster paint is not washable.

You might want the napkin rings to be waterproof. You probably won't plan to wash the bracelet or piggy bank.

2. You'll want the first layer of paint to be dark or heavy enough to cover the newsprint in the paper. If you plan to use acrylic paints, a white emulsion will do this well. Any dark paint will cover better than a light paint. Use old or inexpensive brushes because they may break on the rough spots in your project.

3. After you've applied the basic color, let it dry thoroughly. If you add a second or third coat, let each coat dry well. Then use a pencil to draw any special design or features that you'd like, such as eyes for the pig. You'll probably have more fun and enjoy your projects more if you add extra designs. Magic Markers will work well to add the different colors for your designs.

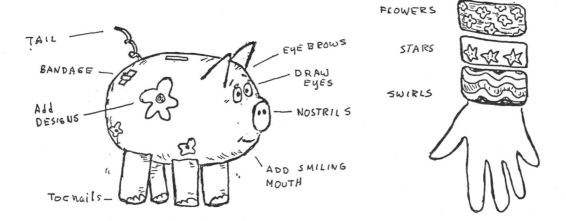

SPECIAL EVENTS

A messsy party

Messy activities for a
hot summer day

A messy party

This is a fun idea for a birthday party or some other special event. If you can't find another excuse for the party, why not just have the party anyway?

Be sure all of the kids and parents know that this is going to be a messy party. The guests will need to wear old clothes and bring a paint shirt. If your Mom or Dad have been saving some old shirts, they may want to have them handy just in case someone forgets or needs to change shirts.

Messy party activities

Choose activities from this book for your guests to enjoy. Some suggestions might include:

- T-Shirt Decorating

- Squishy but No-mess Finger Painting

- Tasty Finger Painting

- Indoor Gardens in individual cans or paper cups

- Clay for Play

Let your guests take home their creations in individual plastic bags.

Messy cake

Let the guests decorate the cake. Use either a sheet cake or individual cupcakes. Buy a spreadable frosting or make your own.

Give each person a popsicle stick or a tongue depressor to use as a spreader. Also buy some tubes of different colored frosting and let each person take turns drawing a decoration. Gum drops, narrow licorice sticks, chocolate chips, sugar sprinkles and animal crackers are also fun decorations.

Sometimes the guests have trouble thinking of ideas so you can write some decorating suggestions on pieces of paper and let each person pick a piece of paper. Suggestions might include:

- Write your name

- Draw an airplane

- Draw a flower

- Or other creative hints.

They should be simple and easy to draw.

When the decorating is finished, of course, everyone gets to eat the cake.

Messy activities for a hot summer day

Big bubbles

You'll need:

- 4 tablespoons glycerine

- 1 1/3 cups dishwashing soap (Joy, Dawn or Ajax)

- 2 gallons water

- A small plastic child's swimming pool

- A dishpan

- A hula hoop and other large forms for bubbles

1. Mix the glycerine, soap and water in the pool. With large loops, squares and other outline forms you can make gigantic bubbles.

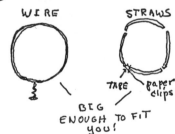

2. Make different shapes from wire or from drinking straws that have string threaded through the straws or are clipped together with wire paper clips and tape.

3. Put the dishpan in the pool. Have a child (or adult) stand in the dry dishpan in the middle of the soapy pool.

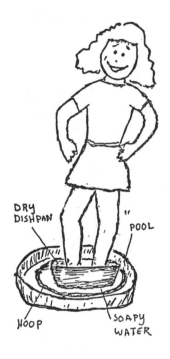

DRY DISHPAN

POOL

HOOP

SOAPY WATER

WOW!

HOOP LIFTED

GIANT BUBBLE

4. Lift the hoop from the soapy pool up over the head of the child and she/he will be standing inside of a bubble. Great fun for everyone!

5. Warning: The hoola hoop works best on a calm day. If the wind blows the bubble against clothing it'll break before it's completed. Be sure to use the dishpan. Otherwise, the child standing in the pool is likely to slip in the soapy water.

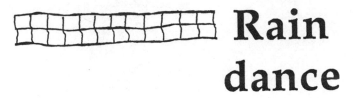 # Rain dance

You'll need

- A water sprinkler

- Handmade rainmaker musical instruments made from:
— Aluminum foil pie pans
— Sand or pebbles
— Old metal pans
— A metal spoon
— Empty plastic detergent bottles
— Empty plastic margarine containers
— Rice
— Beans

On a hot day, a little rain would always feel good. In the past, many people have used dance as a way of asking for rain. Why not try to make your own raindance?

1. You can compose your own raindance and dance in the spray from the water sprinkler.

2. Make your musical instruments. Old metal pans make a great noise if you hit them with the metal spoon. Knock two metal pans against each other for cymbals. Sand in aluminum foil pie pans makes a swishing sound. Pebbles will rattle.

3. Add rice or beans to the detergent bottles and margarine containers, then shake them.

SHAKE!

SHAKE!

BEANS
IN
Detergent
bottle

BAM!

BAM!

Rattle

Rattle

Dance!

Dance!

OH! OH!

Pebbles
in Pan

Metal spoon
on pan

4. Dance in the water as it squirts out from the sprinkler. Provide rhythm with your musical instruments. Have a wonderful wet time.

Water balloons

You'll need

- Balloons

- A faucet or hose connected to a faucet

1. Fill the balloons with water from the hose or faucet. Tie the end of the balloon by knotting it or by tying it tightly with a piece of string. You may need a helper for this.

HOSE

BALLOON

FILL!

FILL!

TIED

2. Play catch with the balloons.

3. You can make a game by seeing how many times a person can catch a water balloon. If you'd like, after every catch, you can step back one pace.

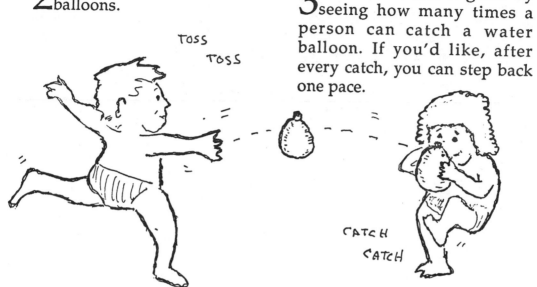

TOSS
TOSS

CATCH
CATCH

4. The person with the most catches wins. But watch out: someone is going to get wet. What fun.

YES!

TOSS
IT
HERE!

DANCE
DANCE

BLOOP!

Other summer day activities

There are a lot of other messy things to do outside. Some suggestions:

1. You can make mud pies or fossils and then wash yourself under the hose, before you go inside.

2. Do splatter or sand painting outside without having to spread newspapers around.